December
Patterns & Projects

Newbridge Educational Publishing, LLC
New York

The purchase of this book entitles the buyer to duplicate
these pages for use by students in the buyer's classroom.
All other permissions must be obtained from the publisher.

© 2000 Newbridge Educational Publishing, LLC,
333 East 38th Street, New York, NY 10016. All rights reserved.

ISBN: 1-58273-128-4

Photo Credit: (cover and title page) Terje Rakke/The Image Bank

Table of Contents

My Snowman Book 5
Snowman Shape Game 9
Snowman Mural 10

The Shoemaker and the Elves Flannel Board 11
The Shoemaker and the Elves Flannel Board Story 12
Find the Matching Shoes 16
Stenciled Greeting Cards 17
Winter Puzzles 21
Trees in Winter Class Discussion 21
Winter Word Rhyme 22
Recommended Reading 22

Menorah Bulletin Board 23
Festival of Lights Flannel Board 27
Festival of Lights Flannel Board Story 28

Hanukkah Art Projects 32
Dreidel, Dreidel, Dreidel 36
Grouping by Eight 37
Hanukkah Song 38
Hanukkah Cookies 39
Class Discussion 40
Recommended Reading 41

Learning About La Posada 42
La Posada Mobile 43
La Posada Cards 47
La Posada Story 48

La Posada Piñata 49
La Posada Story Sequencing 53
Piñata Song 54

Santa Claus Paper-Bag Puppet 55
Santa Song 59
Santa Claus Maze 60

Reindeer Stick Puppets 61
Snowflake Crowns 61
Counting by Twos 63
Reindeer and Snowflake Counting Game 63
Reindeer Weather Calendar 64

Table of Contents (continued)

Holiday Ornaments 65
Christmas Mice Decorations 67
Guess the Gifts 69

The Values of Kwanzaa 71
Kwanzaa Holiday Cards 72
Kwanzaa Idea Chart 76
Kwanzaa Place Mats 76
Kwanzaa Pendant Necklaces 78
African-Style Hats 78

MY SNOWMAN BOOK

Share the storybook *The Snowman* by Raymond Briggs, published by Random House, with your class. Then help children make up their own stories about snowmen.

You need:
- scissors
- white construction paper
- glue
- crayons or markers
- glitter
- 12" x 18" construction paper
- stapler

1. Reproduce the snowman patterns on pages 6 through 8 once for each child and cut out.
2. Help each child cut out an 8" circle from white construction paper to make the snowman's body.
3. Have each child assemble a snowman by gluing the head onto the body, the hat onto the head, and the accessories in place, as shown.
4. Let children decorate their snowmen using crayons or markers and glitter.
5. Give each child six 12" x 18" pieces of construction paper. Have children staple the paper together to make a book.
6. Ask children to glue their snowmen to the covers of their books. Then have children make up their own stories about snowmen by illustrating each page in the book. Children may also want to write or dictate text to go along with their illustrations.
7. Over the course of a week, let each child present his or her snowman story to the class.

Step 3

Snowman Hat Pattern

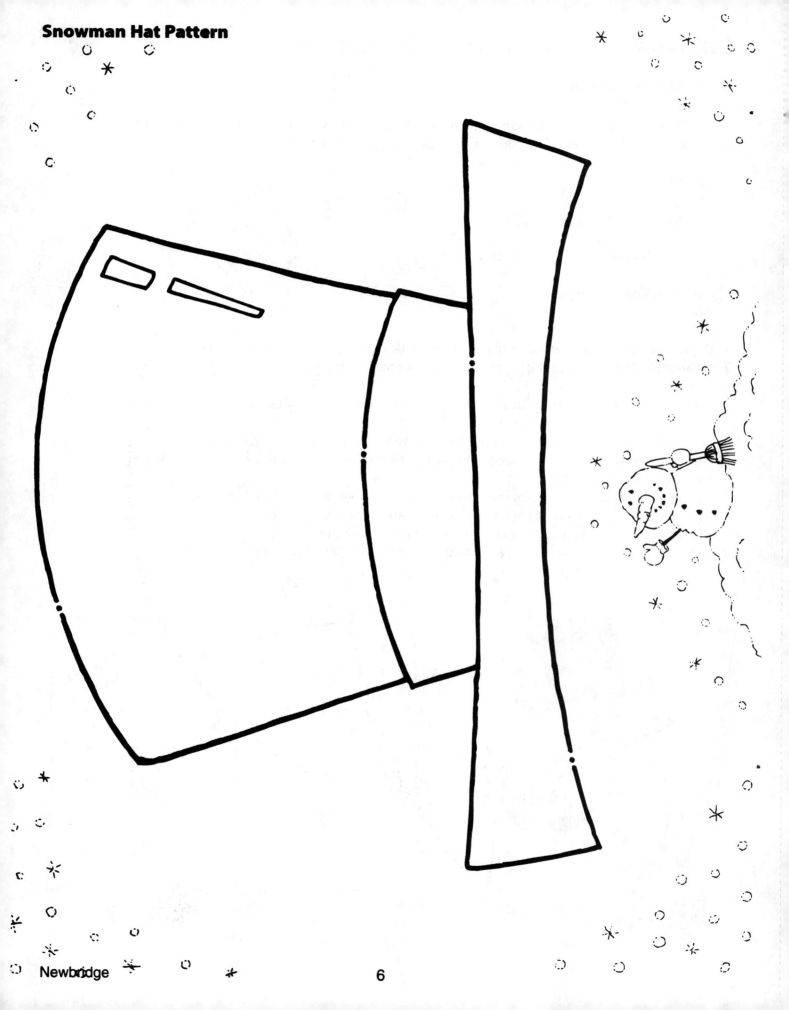

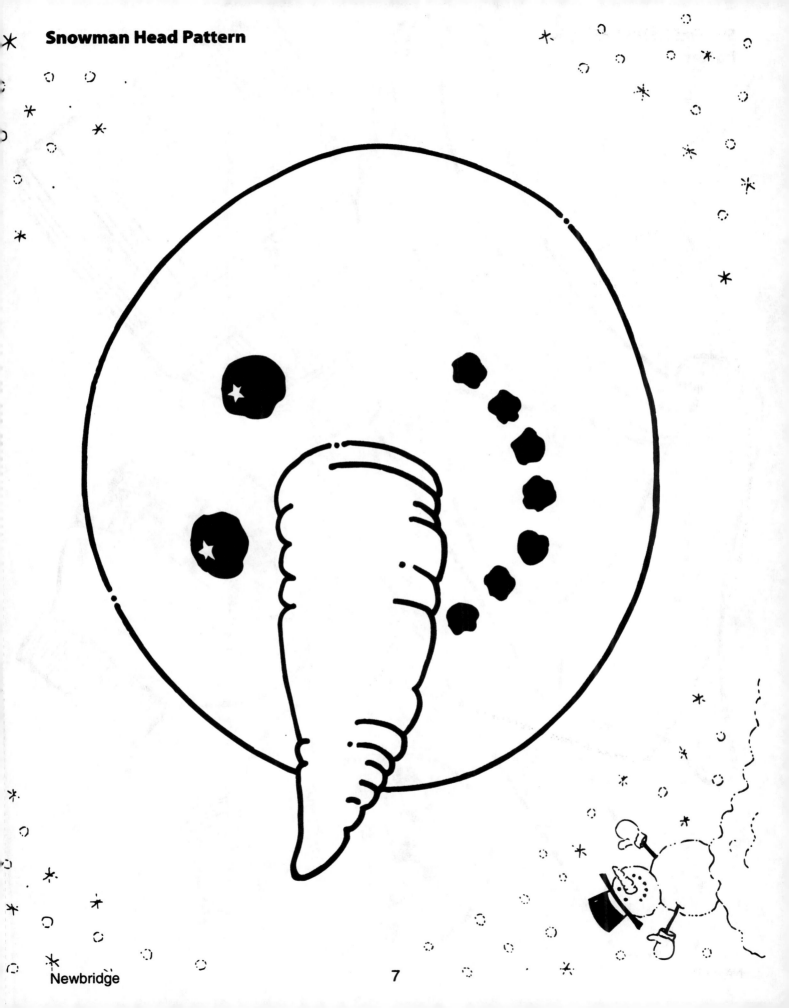

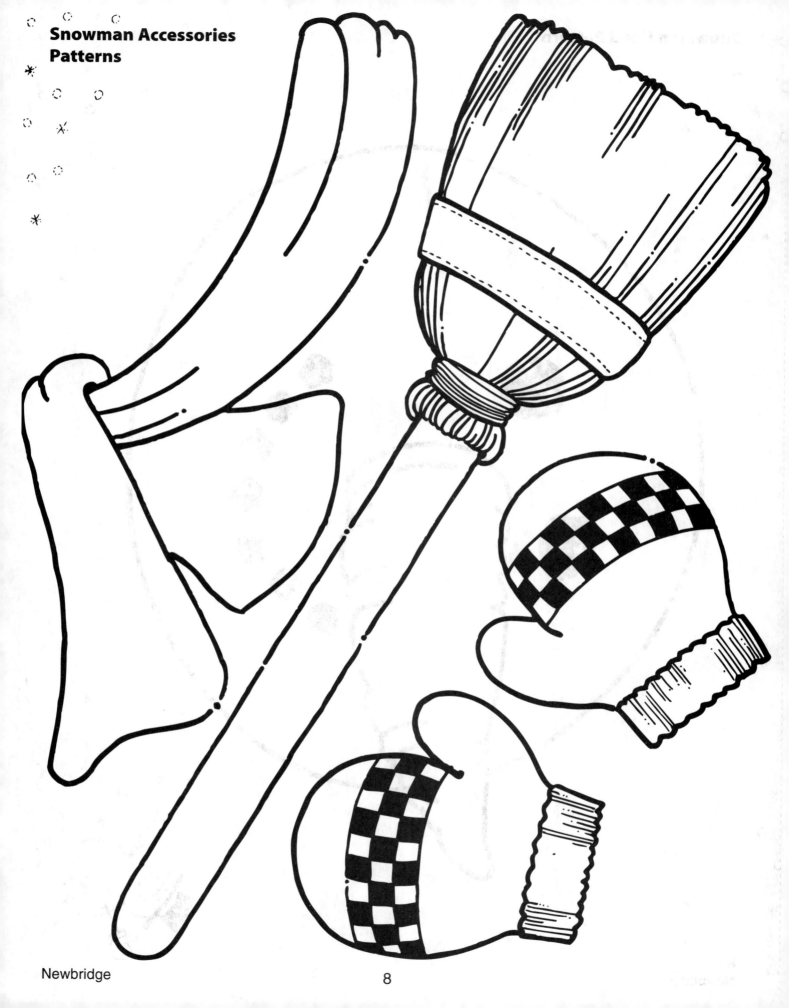

SNOWMAN SHAPE GAME

You need:
- white felt
- scissors
- colored felt

1. Using white felt, cut out a 6", 8", and 10" circle to make the snowman's head and body.
2. Cut small triangles, circles, squares, and rectangles out of the colored felt to use for facial features and buttons.
3. Using colored felt, cut out a 5" square and a 1" x 8" rectangle to make a hat, and a triangle with a 5" base and a 1" x 12" rectangle to make a broom
4. Place the felt snowman in the middle of a flannel board. Place the felt shapes around the edges of the flannel board.
5. In small groups, ask children, one at a time, to follow your instructions to add facial features, buttons, hat, and broom to the snowman. For example, you might say, "Put on circle eyes" or "Put on square buttons."
6. Continue until the snowman is complete. Let children play with the flannel board during free time to make their own shape snowman.

CIRCLE SQUARE TRIANGLE RECT

SNOWMAN MURAL

You need:
- tape
- large mural paper
- brown paint and brushes
- crayons or markers
- scissors
- glue
- wooden spoon
- soap flakes
- water
- mixing bowl

1. Tape 10 feet of large mural paper to a classroom wall.
2. Divide the class into three groups—Trees, Snowmen, and Children—to work on the mural at different times.
3. Ask the Trees group to paint several large brown tree trunks and branches on the mural paper.
4. Then have the Snowmen group assemble and decorate several snowmen (see page 5, steps 1 through 4) and glue them to the mural.
5. Ask the Children group to draw pictures of children.
6. Using a wooden spoon, mix four parts soap flakes with one part water in a large mixing bowl.
7. Let all children use the soap flake mixture and take turns finger-painting "snow" on the ground, trees, and snowmen. (The mixture will stick by itself to the mural.)
8. Title the mural "Our Snowman Friends." On a piece of paper, have each child write or dictate a sentence telling what he or she would do with a snowman friend. Attach the papers around the mural.

THE SHOEMAKER AND THE ELVES FLANNEL BOARD

You need:
- scissors
- flannel
- crayons or markers
- glue

1. Reproduce the shoemaker and the elves patterns on pages 13 through 15 and cut out.
2. Trace the figures and clothes on pieces of flannel and cut out. Or, color the paper figures and glue small pieces of flannel to the backs of the clothes and the backs and fronts of the figures.
3. Move the figures around a flannel board as you read "The Shoemaker and the Elves" on page 12.
4. For additional props, you may want to add scraps of flannel to represent the pieces of leather the shoemaker puts out each night, and a 9" x 12" piece of flannel to make the curtain the shoemaker and his wife hide behind.
5. Later, place the flannel board and figures where children can use them to retell the story or make up their own stories featuring these characters.

THE SHOEMAKER AND THE ELVES FLANNEL BOARD STORY

Once upon a time, a shoemaker and his wife lived in a little village. Although they were good people who worked very hard, there came a time when business was bad. At the end of one day, the shoemaker and his wife discovered they only had one piece of leather left, and no money to buy any more. The shoemaker sadly cut the piece of leather and placed it on his workbench so he would be ready to work the next morning. Then he and his wife went to bed, wondering how they would live after the last pair of shoes was sold.

The next morning, they woke up early, ready to work. But when the shoemaker walked over to the workbench, what did he see but a pair of the finest shoes ever made!

Just then a man came into the shop. When the man saw the shoes on the workbench, he insisted he must have them. The man paid a fine price for the beautiful shoes, and he asked the shoemaker to make him another pair for the next day. The shoemaker was delighted, and he immediately went out and bought enough leather to make two pairs of shoes.

That evening, the shoemaker again cut the leather and placed the pieces on the workbench. But the next morning, as soon as he walked into the workshop, he discovered two pairs of shoes on the workbench. These shoes were even more beautiful than the first pair!

The man returned and bought both pairs of shoes. The shoemaker went right out and bought enough leather to make four pairs of shoes. He cut the leather and put it on his workbench, just as he did every night. And what do you think he found the next morning? Four pairs of shoes were waiting for him.

By now, the people in town had heard about the wonderful shoes, and everyone wanted a pair. Each evening the shoemaker cut more leather, and each morning he found more and more wonderful shoes on his workbench.

The shoemaker and his wife were so thankful for their good fortune that they decided to stay up one night and find out who was making the lovely shoes. They hid behind a curtain in the shop and waited. They waited and waited. Finally, as the clock struck midnight, they heard little feet running about. The shoemaker and his wife slowly peeked out from behind the curtain. What did they see but two elves dressed only in long underwear, climbing up on the workbench. The two little elves worked and worked until the shoes were finished. Then they ran away as quickly as they had come.

The shoemaker and his wife decided to show the elves how grateful they were for their help. The next day, the shoemaker made a tiny pair of shoes for each elf, and his wife sewed some tiny clothes for them.

That night, the shoemaker and his wife placed the clothes and shoes on the workbench. Then they hid behind the curtain. Just as the clock struck midnight, the elves returned. When they saw the tiny clothes and shoes on the workbench they squealed with delight. They quickly put the clothes and shoes on and danced about. They played and sang for hours until the sun began to rise. Then the little elves quickly ran away.

The shoemaker and his wife never saw the elves again, but their business grew and grew. And they were always happy because they had been able to show the elves how thankful they were for their help.

The Shoemaker and the Elves Flannel Board Patterns

The Shoemaker and the Elves Flannel Board Patterns

FIND THE MATCHING SHOES

Help the elves find the matching shoes. Cut out the pictures at the bottom of the page and paste each shoe next to one that is exactly the same.

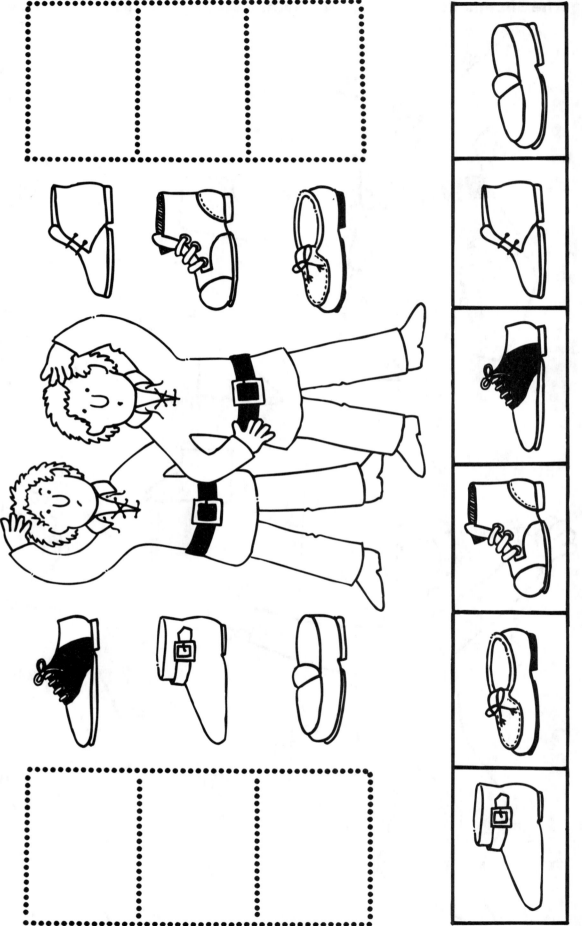

Newbridge

STENCILED GREETING CARDS

You need:
- scissors
- 12" x 18" construction paper
- chalk
- tissues or paper towels
- crayons or markers

1. Divide the class into pairs. Let each pair select a pattern on pages 18 through 20 to use for a greeting card. Reproduce the selected pattern once for each pair and cut out.
2. Fold a piece of 12" x 18" construction paper in half for each pair. Have children use the card patterns as stencils by tracing the figures onto the construction paper with chalk, as shown.
3. Tell children to hold their stencils in place on the construction paper. Using tissues or paper towels, ask children to rub the chalk from the edges of the stencils out onto the construction paper, as shown.
4. Remove the stencil and discard. Have children use crayons or markers to decorate the cards. Ask each pair to write or dictate a message for a school helper (such as a librarian, cafeteria worker, or principal) on the inside of the card. Discuss why people like to give and receive cards, and the importance of letting someone know he or she is appreciated.
5. Have pairs sign their card, then hand-deliver the card to the school helper.

Step 2

Step 3

Stenciled Greeting Card Pattern

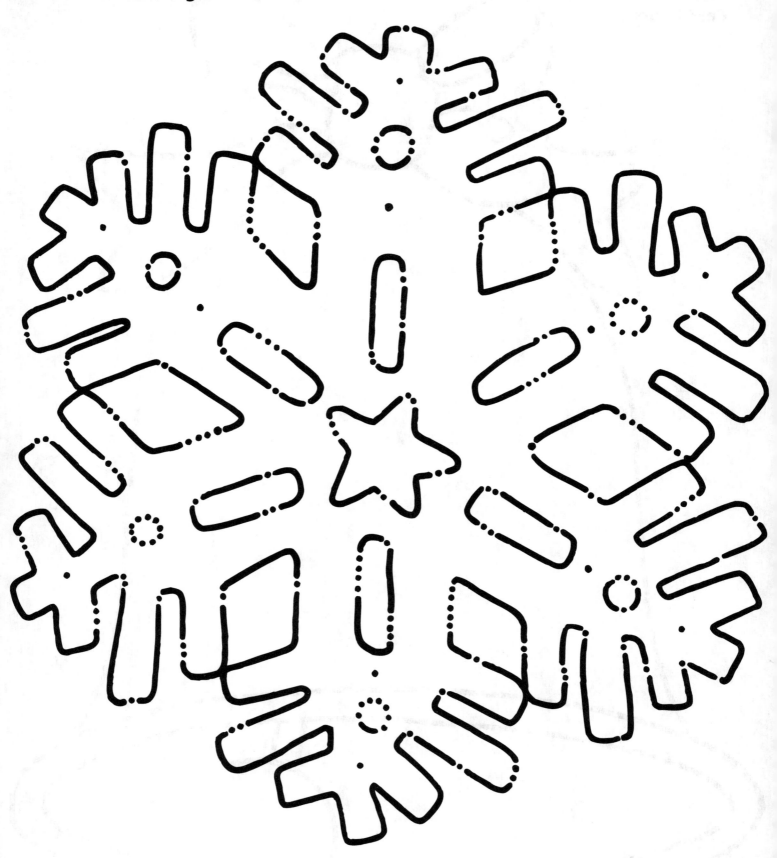

WINTER PUZZLES

1. Reproduce the tree, bell, and snowflake patterns on pages 18 through 20 once. Color, laminate, and cut out.
2. Cut each figure into five or six puzzle pieces, as shown. Place each set of puzzle pieces in an envelope. Allow children to assemble the puzzles during free time.

TREES IN WINTER CLASS DISCUSSION

Read *The Fir Tree* by Hans Christian Andersen (published by HarperCollins) to your class. Then take the class outside to observe trees in the winter. Ask students if the trees look different from the way they did in the summer. Explain that Christmas trees are called evergreens because they stay green all year long. Show the class needles from a pine tree. Tell children that even though these needles look strange, they are actually leaves. The leaves on an evergreen are just a different shape from the leaves on other trees. This shape helps prevent the leaves from drying out in the autumn the way other leaves do. Ask children to gather pinecones, evergreen branches, and other objects to take back to the classroom to observe. If desired, have children write or draw an experience story about trees in winter.

WINTER WORD RHYME

1. Reproduce the bell, tree, and snowflake patterns on pages 18 through 20 once. Label them "BELL," "TREE," and "SNOW," as shown.
2. Divide the class into several small groups. Reproduce the labeled figures once for each group and cut out.
3. Have each group glue their figure onto a large piece of construction paper.
4. Ask each group to write or dictate all the words they can think of that rhyme with the word on each piece of construction paper.
5. When everyone is finished, call on children to read aloud the words they have listed. See if anyone has thought of a word that no one else has.

CELL
DELL
FELL

ME
FREE
SEE

KNOW
BLOW
GLOW

RECOMMENDED READING

Read the following winter storybooks to your class. Place the books on a reading table or in a bookcase so that children may look at them during free time.

Geraldine's Big Snow by Holly Keller, published by Greenwillow.
Katy and the Big Snow by Virginia Lee Burton, published by Houghton Mifflin.
Little Fur Family by Margaret Wise Brown, published by HarperCollins.
The Mitten by Alvin Tresselt, published by Lothrop, Lee & Shepard.
Morris' Disappearing Bag by Rosemary Wells, published by Dial Press.
The Polar Express by Chris Van Allsburg, published by Houghton Mifflin.
The Snowy Day by Ezra Jack Keats, published by Viking Peguin.
White Snow Bright Snow by Alvin Tresselt, published by William Morrow.

MENORAH BULLETIN BOARD

You need:
- crayons or markers
- scissors
- glue
- white oaktag
- envelope
- tape

1. Reproduce the menorah patterns on pages 24 and 25 once. Reproduce the candle and flame patterns on page 26 three times. Color and cut.
2. Glue the two pieces of the menorah together onto a piece of white oaktag, as shown.
3. Glue one candle on each menorah candleholder, as shown.
4. Place the flames in an envelope. Attach the envelope to the bottom of the oaktag.
5. Display the poster on a classroom wall or bulletin board. On the first day of Hanukkah, tape one flame over the center candle, called the *shamash*, and one flame over the first candle on the left. Each day, tape another flame on a candle, moving from left to right across the menorah.
6. Use the information from the "Festival of Lights" story on page 28 to explain the significance of this bulletin board to children.

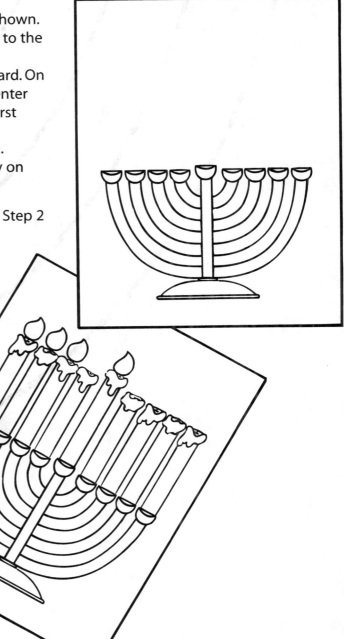

Step 2

Step 3

Menorah Pattern

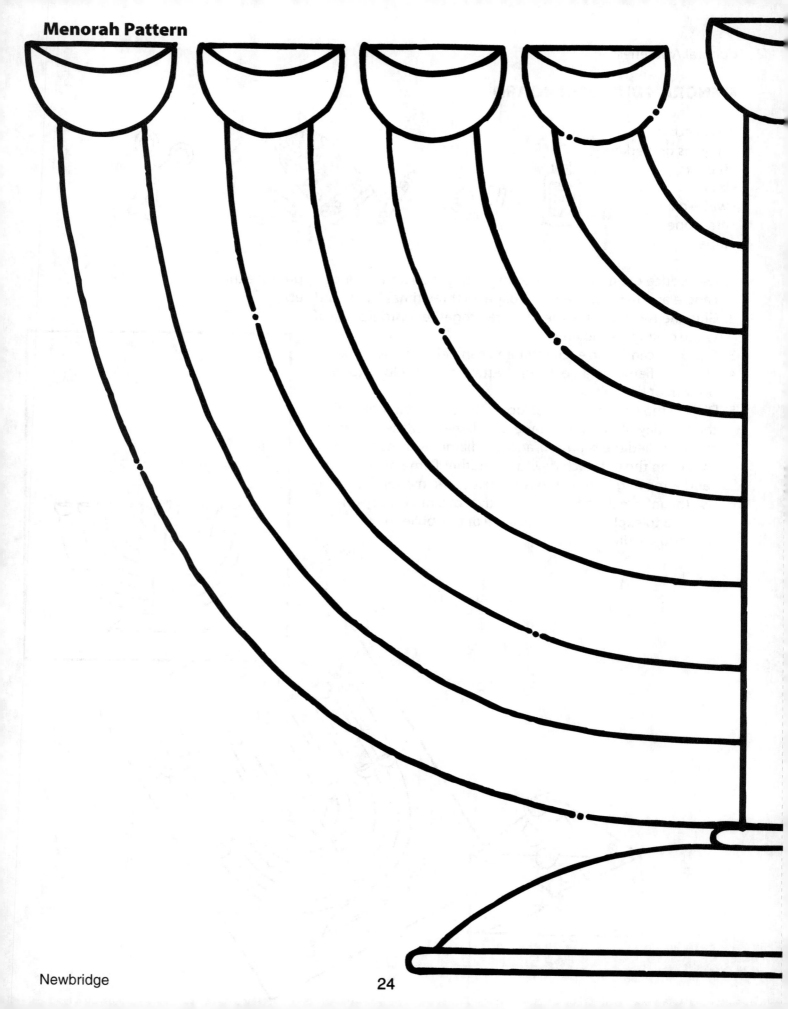

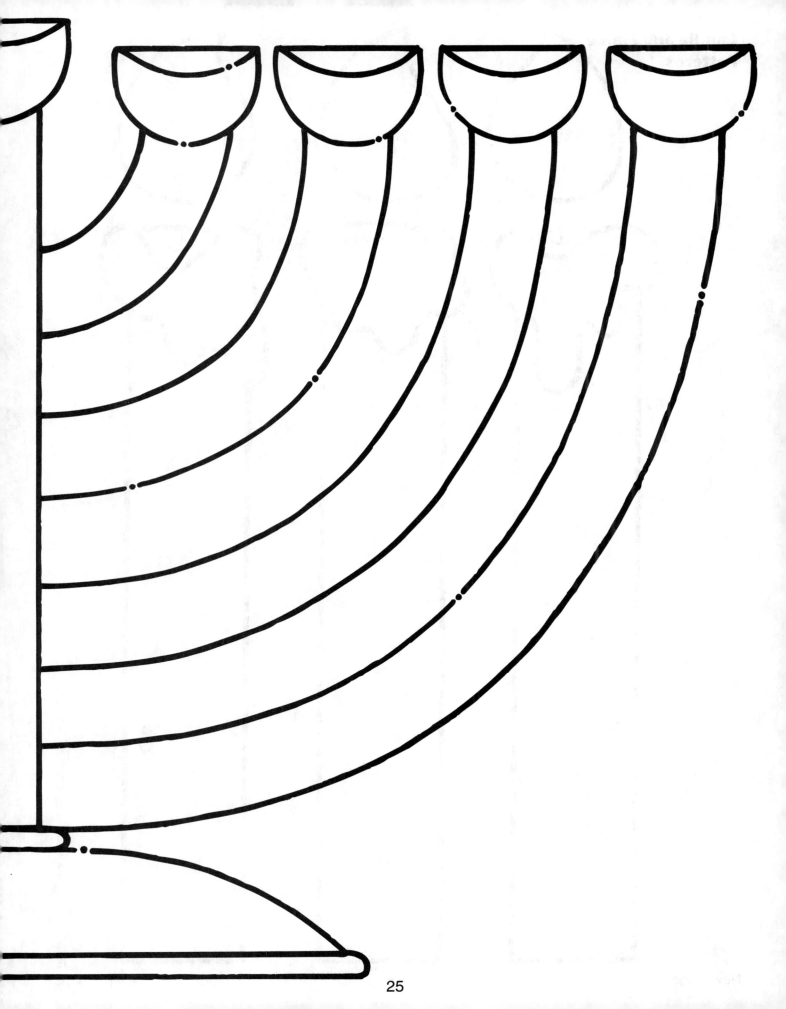

FESTIVAL OF LIGHTS FLANNEL BOARD

You need:
• crayons or markers
• oaktag
• glue
• scissors
• sandpaper scraps

1. Reproduce all the flannel board patterns on pages 29 through 31 once. Have volunteers color, mount on oaktag, and cut out.
2. Glue small scraps of sandpaper to the backs of the figures.
3. Move the figures around the flannel board as you read the "Festival of Lights" story on page 28.
4. Leave the flannel board figures out so that children can retell the story during free time.

FESTIVAL OF LIGHTS
FLANNEL BOARD STORY

A very, very long time ago, a group of people built a temple, a place to worship that was very important to them. The people were Jews, and the temple was in a city called Jerusalem.

One day another group of people, led by a king named Antiochus, made the Jews leave their temple. This made the Jews very sad, but they met secretly to figure out a way to get the temple back.

A man named Judah Maccabee got together with a group of followers and fought the king's army. After a long battle, the Maccabees won. They earned back the right to use their temple.

When the Jews went back to the place in Jerusalem where the temple was, they were horrified. The temple was almost ruined! This made the Jews very angry because the temple had been so important to their lives. They set to work and started to clean and fix up the temple. This huge task took them many days, but at last they were finished. They decided to hold a small celebration to honor their temple once again.

The Jews had a special lamp they used in the temple. But they could find only one jar of oil to use as fuel for the lamp. So they lit the lamp and stayed in the temple. When one day was up, the oil should have been used up, too. But the people noticed that the oil was still burning. In fact, the oil burned for eight days. The Jewish people thought it was a miracle! And they promised never to forget the miracle of the lamp that burned for eight days.

Their remembrance of that time so long ago is why people celebrate Hanukkah. Jewish families today light eight candles on a menorah, which is a special candleholder to remind them of the great festival of lights.

Festival of Lights Patterns

HANUKKAH ART PROJECTS

You need:
- crayons or markers
- scissors
- glue
- 12" x 18" oaktag
- clear contact paper
- glitter
- large cotton balls
- stapler

1. Reproduce the place mat pattern on pages 34 and 35 once for each child. Have children color and cut out. Then have them mount the mat on a 12" x 18" piece of oaktag. Children may draw their own picture in the middle. Laminate the place mats, which children may give as gifts.

2. Reproduce the greeting card pattern on page 33 for each child. Children may color their cards and add glitter if they like. Then have children mount on oaktag. Help children fold their cards and write a message to a friend.

3. Reproduce the dreidel pattern on page 33 once for each child. Have children color, cut out, and mount on oaktag. Help children staple the dreidel at the tab and along the bottom, leaving a space to put a pencil through, as shown. Help children stuff the dreidel with cotton while they hold the pencil in place. Then show how to spin the dreidel.

Step 3

Dreidel and Card Patterns

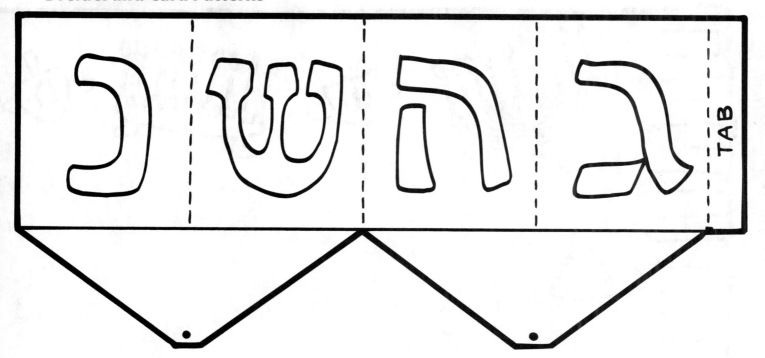

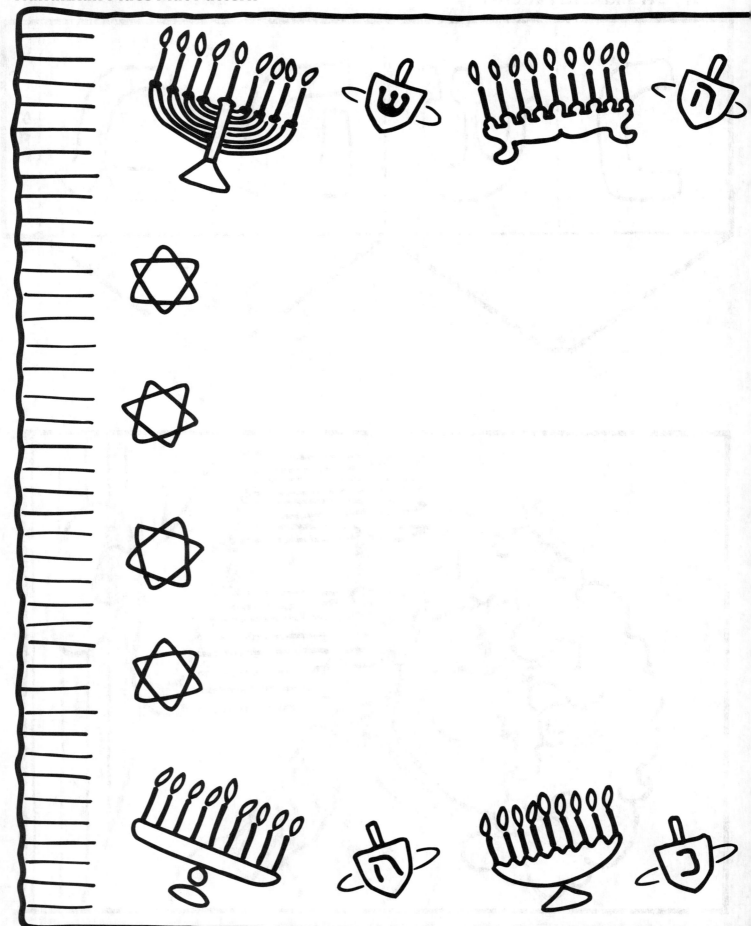

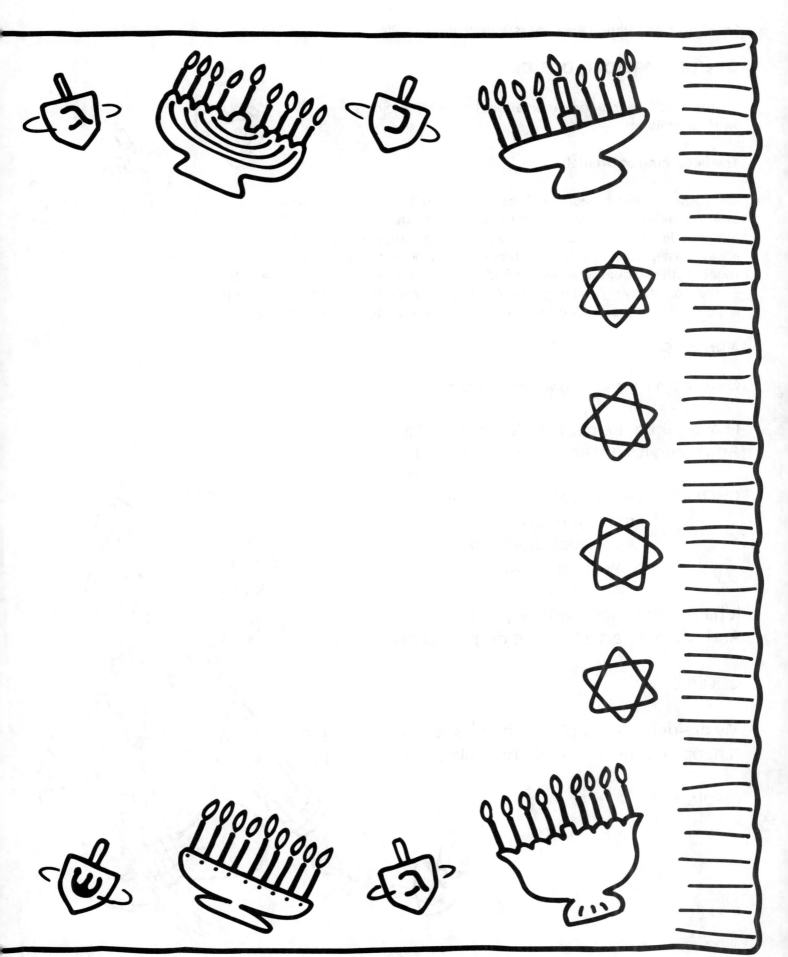

DREIDEL, DREIDEL, DREIDEL

Share the following information about Hanukkah dreidels with the children.

The Beginning of Dreidels

Long ago the Jewish people in Israel were ruled by the Syrians. The Syrian king ordered the Jews to give up their religion and follow the Syrian religion instead. Studying Jewish laws and customs was no longer allowed. But Jewish children found a way to keep up their religious studies secretly. When Syrian soldiers saw the children together, they would walk over to find out what they were doing. The Jewish children would stop studying and begin to play an innocent game with a spinning top called a dreidel. When the soldiers left, the children would return to their studies.

A Dreidel Song

Children can sing this song while spinning their dreidels.

I have a little dreidel, I made it out of clay,
And when it's dry and ready, oh dreidel I will play!

CHORUS: Oh, dreidel, dreidel, dreidel,
               I made it out of clay,
               Oh, dreidel, dreidel, dreidel,
               Now dreidel I will play.

It has a lovely body, with leg so short and thin,
And when it gets all tired, it drops and then I win!

CHORUS

My dreidel's always playful, it loves to dance and spin,
A happy game of dreidel, come play, now let's begin!

CHORUS

GROUPING BY EIGHT

Because the Hanukkah oil burned for eight days, the holiday of Hanukkah is eight days long. Children can focus on the number 8 with the following two activities.

1. Have children work with a partner or small group to find classroom items to group by eight. For example, they might group 8 rubber bands, 8 books, 8 shoes, or 8 pieces of paper. Later, invite children to display their groups for the class and to count aloud the items in each group.
2. Have children think of words that rhyme with *eight*. List their suggestions on the chalkboard or on a sheet of oaktag. Your list might include the following:

   date, gate, late, great, Kate, plate, straight, wait, weight, state, skate, freight…

3. Invite volunteers to make up sentences using the words from the list.

HANUKKAH SONG

Teach your class the following Hanukkah action song. Children may also enjoy playing along with such rhythm instruments as finger cymbals, triangles, and bells.

Hanukkah (Jewish Folk Tune)

1. Ha – nuk – kah,   Ha – nuk – kah,   fes- ti- val of lights!
   (clap hands to beat)
2. Ha – nuk – kah,   Ha – nuk – kah,   what a mer – ry time!
   (clap hands to beat)

1. Can – dles glow in a row, sev – en days, eight nights.
   (hold up four fingers on each hand)
2. Cakes to eat, what a treat, see the fac – es shine!
   (smile broadly)

1. Ha – nuk – kah,   Ha – nuk – kah,   make your drei – del spin,
   (clap hands to beat)
2. Ha – nuk – kah,   Ha – nuk – kah,   sing and dance this way,
   (clap hands to beat)

1. Round and round, round and round, ev – ery – one join in!
   (spin around)
2. Round and round, round and round, hap – py hol – i –day!
   (spin around)

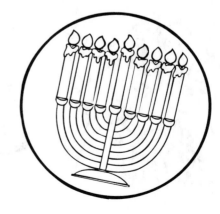

HANUKKAH COOKIES

You need:
- rolling pin
- knife
- cookie sheet
- sugar cookie dough
 (from prepared mix or refrigerated tubes)
- canned lemon frosting
- tubes of decorating icing

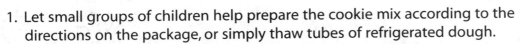

1. Let small groups of children help prepare the cookie mix according to the directions on the package, or simply thaw tubes of refrigerated dough.
2. Have two children roll out the dough until it is about 1/2" thick.
3. Show children how to make candle-shaped cookies by cutting out a long, thin rectangle, a small triangle, and a circle.
4. Bake cookies according to the directions. When the cookies are done, allow them to cool and let children frost them using canned lemon frosting. Give children tubes of decorating icing to decorate the cookies.

CLASS DISCUSSION

After reading "Festival of Lights" on page 28, have a class discussion about Hanukkah and its traditions. Ask if anyone in the class has a menorah at home. Explain that every year at Hanukkah, Jewish families light a candle on the menorah each night in memory of the lights that burned for eight nights in the temple of Jerusalem. Ask volunteers to describe how their families celebrate Hanukkah, what foods they eat, what games they play (dreidel), and what kinds of special family traditions they follow. Tell the class that many families celebrate Hanukkah by giving gifts to each other on each of the eight nights.

RECOMMENDED READING

Read some of the following books about Hanukkah to the class. Place the books on a reading table or in a bookcase so that children may look at them during free time.

All About Hanukkah by Judye Groner and Madeline Wikler, published by Kar-Ben.
A Chanukah Fable for Christmas by Jerome Coopersmith, published by Putnam.
Hanukkah by June Behrens, published by Children's Press.
Hanukkah by Norma Simon, published by HarperCollins.
Hanukkah Money by Sholom Aleichem, published by Greenwillow.
I Love Hanukkah by Marilyn Hirsh, published by Holiday House.
Laughing Latkes by M. B. Goffstein, published by Farrar, Straus and Giroux.
A Picture Book of Hanukkah by David A. Adler, published by Holiday House.

LEARNING ABOUT LA POSADA

Share with the class that the English meaning of La Posada is "the ceremony." La Posada is a happy religious holiday celebrated by Mexicans and Mexican-Americans. It is celebrated over a span of nine days. On each of the nine days before Christmas, friends and neighbors gather together for a special ceremony that includes lighting candles, singing songs, and visiting with one another.

Groups of people act out the story of Mary and Joseph and their journey to Jerusalem. They hold a march in memory of that trip. Then figures of Mary and Joseph are placed in the family's *nacimientos*, or manger scene, by a child in the group.

In addition to the religious festivities, the children also play a piñata game. A *piñata* is a clay pot decorated with beautiful colored tissue paper to look like a toy animal. It is stuffed with nuts, fruits, toys, and *dulce*, a kind of candy children are given only on special occasions. It is then hung way up in the air over the children's heads. The children take turns being blindfolded and trying to break the piñata with a stick. When it is broken, they gather up all the treats that have fallen out.

LA POSADA MOBILE

You need:
• crayons or markers
• scissors
• yarn
• stapler
• hangers

1. Reproduce the patterns on pages 44 through 46 once for each child. Have children color and cut out.
2. Take lengths of yarn approximately 30" each and staple one end of each piece of yarn to a pattern, as shown.
3. Tie the other end of each piece of yarn to the base of a wire hanger, as shown.
4. Suspend the hanger from the ceiling. Open the windows so the wind can blow each of the mobiles.

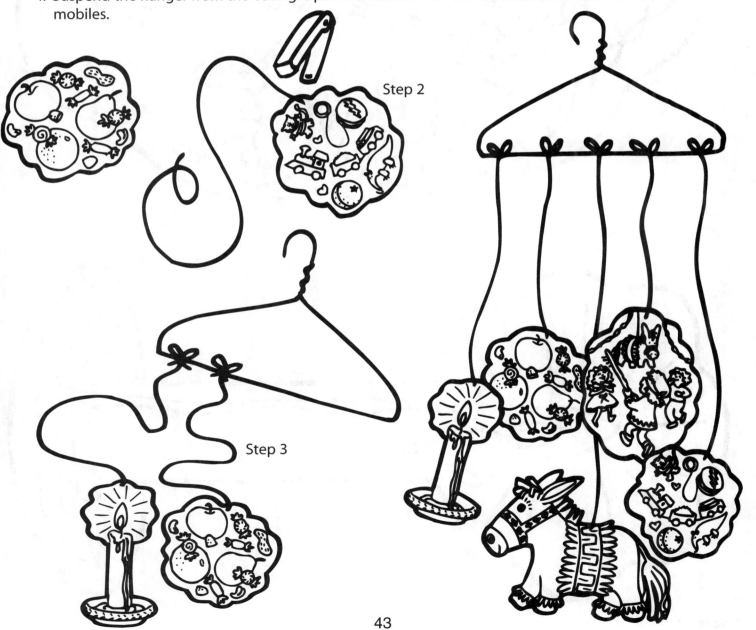

Step 2

Step 3

La Posada Mobile Patterns

LA POSADA CARDS

You need:
• crayons or markers
• scissors
• 8-1/2" x 11" paper (one piece for each child)
• glue
• glitter, yarn, ribbon

1. Have each child choose a favorite pattern from pages 44 through 46 and reproduce it for him or her.
2. Have children color their patterns and cut them out.
3. Ask each child to fold a piece of paper to make a card.
4. Have them glue their chosen pattern on the front of the card.
5. Have children write a special holiday message on the inside of the card.
6. Children may add glitter, yarn, or ribbon to the card for additional decoration.

LA POSADA STORY

Carlos and Maria ran out of their house and jumped into their uncle Juan's car. He was taking them to the huge marketplace in town. There they would buy everything their grandmother needed for tonight's posada.

The two cousins walked with Uncle Juan through the market, looking at all the bright mats and clothing people had brought to sell. Their uncle bought them each some *dulce*, a kind of candy they were only given on special occasions. Uncle Juan also bought nuts, candied fruit, and lots of little toys. All these things would go into the piñata they were making for the posada.

When they got to Grandma's house, Carlos and Maria began decorating the piñata. They put all the candies and toys in a clay pot. Then they covered the pot with beautiful colored tissue paper. When it was finished, Uncle Juan hung it way up in the air, over Carlos's and Maria's heads.

When it began to get dark, the children stood by the window. Soon they saw a light coming closer and closer. The children could see many people holding candles. Maria held her breath as she heard a knock on the door.

Carlos opened the door and was greeted by the songs of their neighbors and friends. A little boy stepped away from the crowd and held up figures of Mary and Joseph. Quietly he asked if Mary and Joseph could stay at the house. Carlos and Maria said, "No!" and everyone in their home sang a song that told the people to go away. But the crowd came closer to the door, singing louder. Again the little boy asked if Mary and Joseph could come in and again he was

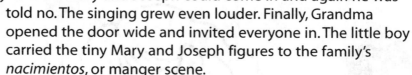

told no. The singing grew even louder. Finally, Grandma opened the door wide and invited everyone in. The little boy carried the tiny Mary and Joseph figures to the family's *nacimientos*, or manger scene.

Out came the cookies and the hot chocolate and the fruit. Everyone sang and laughed and talked, and the children stood around the piñata. Uncle Juan blindfolded a child, and the child swung at the beautiful piñata with a stick. Because they were the hosts of the posada, Carlos and Maria took their turns last. Maria was so excited that the stick trembled in her hand. She swung above her head and the piñata went CRACK! The clay pot shattered, and all the toys and candies spilled out. Posadas were held every evening for the nine days before Christmas. Tomorrow night would be another posada at a neighbor's house. Maria and Carlos looked at each other happily. La Posada was the best holiday of all!

LA POSADA PIÑATA

You need:
- crayons or markers
- scissors
- glue
- oaktag
- stapler
- treats (edible and nonedible)
- hole puncher
- 60" length of yarn
- blindfold
- yardstick

Step 2

1. Reproduce the bull's head on page 50, the body on page 51, and the legs and tail patterns on page 52 twice. Color the front (printed) side of one set and the back (unprinted) side of the other set. Cut out.
2. Glue the head and legs to the bull's body on each set, as shown. Then mount each side on oaktag and cut out.
3. Staple around the edges of the figure, leaving a space open at the top. This creates a pocket inside the bull's body.
4. Fill the pocket with small treats for the class. Then staple the top closed.
5. Punch a hole in the top of the bull. Thread a 60" length of yarn through the hole and string the piñata from the ceiling, as shown, making sure it hangs at a height just above children's heads.
6. Let children take turns being blindfolded and trying to hit the piñata with a yardstick during a class La Posada party.

Step 3

Step 5

49

Bull Head Pattern

Bull Body Pattern

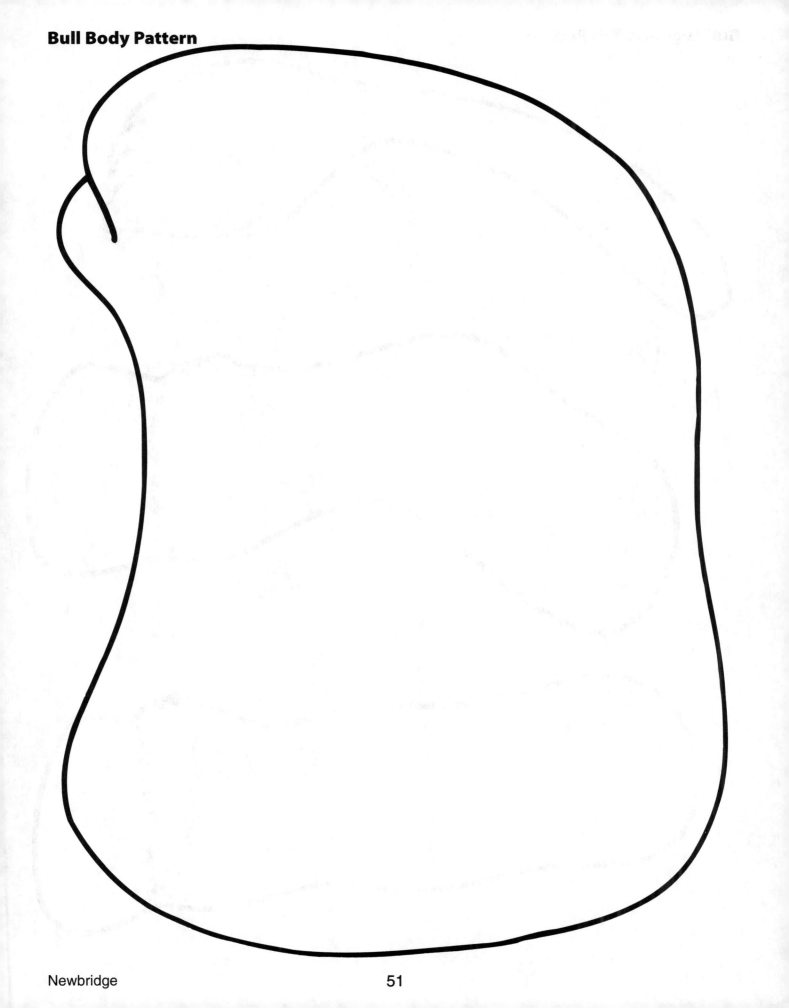

Bull Legs and Tail Patterns

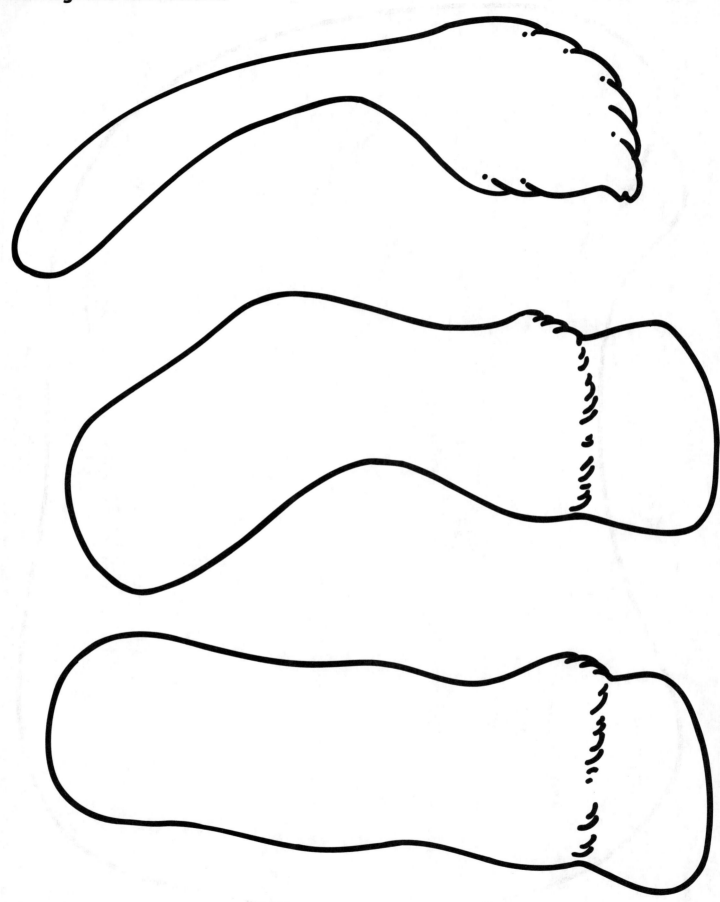

LA POSADA STORY SEQUENCING

Think about the story of Carlos and Maria's posada. Write a number 1 in the box that shows what happened first, a number 2 in the box that shows what happened next, and so on. Color all the pictures.

Name _____

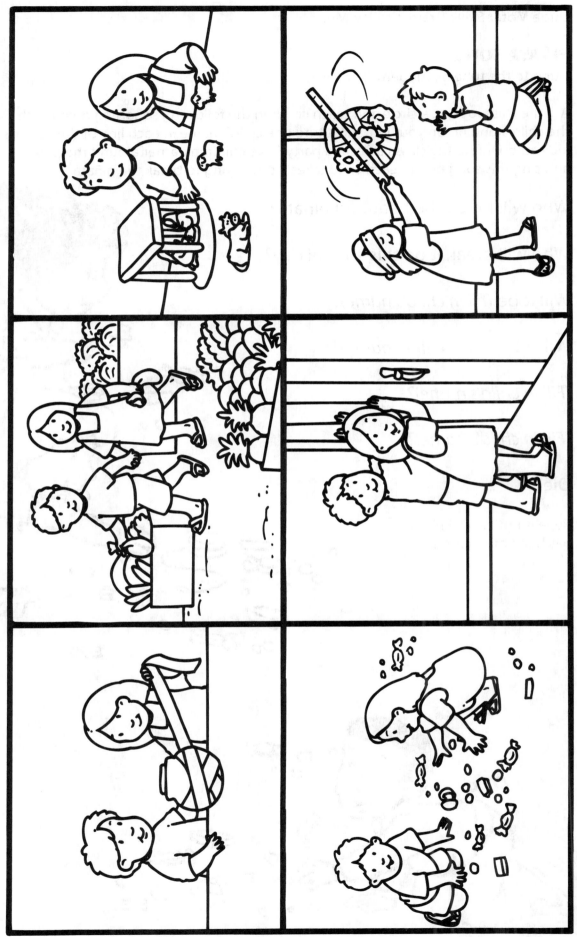

Newbridge

PIÑATA SONG
(sung to the tune of "Alouette")

Ask the class to form a circle and teach children the following song. Beginning with the child standing on your left, substitute one child's name in each line of the song as indicated. During the class La Posada party, have children gather around the piñata and sing this song before each child takes a turn trying to break the piñata.

Who will break the beautiful piñata?

Who will break it on this special day?

Will it be *(fill in child's name)*?

Will it be *(fill in child's name)*?

(Fill in child's name)?

(Fill in child's name)?

Ole!

Repeat until each child's name has been mentioned.

SANTA CLAUS PAPER-BAG PUPPET

You need:
- crayons or markers
- scissors
- glue
- medium-sized brown paper bags (one for each child)
- buttons, ribbons, glitter

1. Reproduce all the Santa patterns on pages 56 through 58 once for each child. Have children color the parts and cut out.
2. Have each child glue the Santa head to the bottom of a medium-sized brown paper bag, as shown.
3. Ask each child to glue the Santa body to the front of the bag, as shown.
4. Have each child glue the boots beneath the body, and the sack over Santa's shoulder, as shown.
5. Encourage each child to personalize his or her puppet by adding buttons, ribbons, glitter, or other available decorating material.

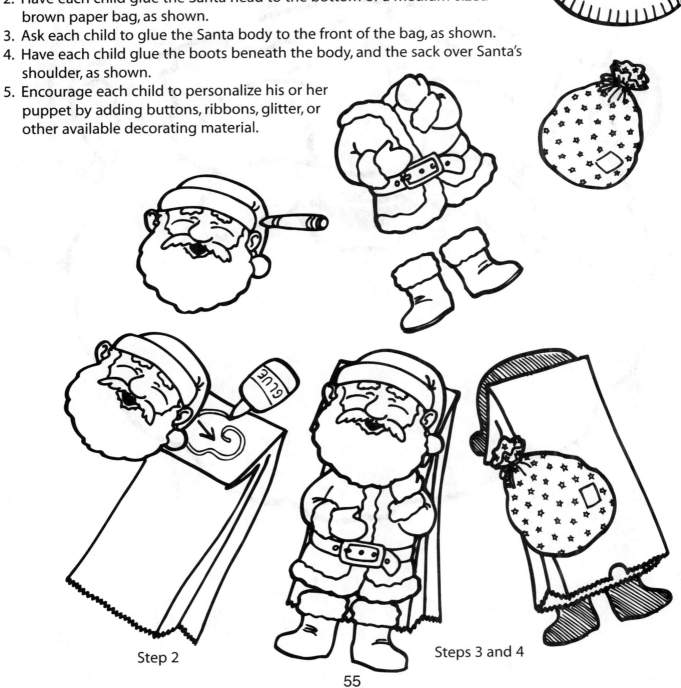

Step 2

Steps 3 and 4

55

Santa Body Pattern

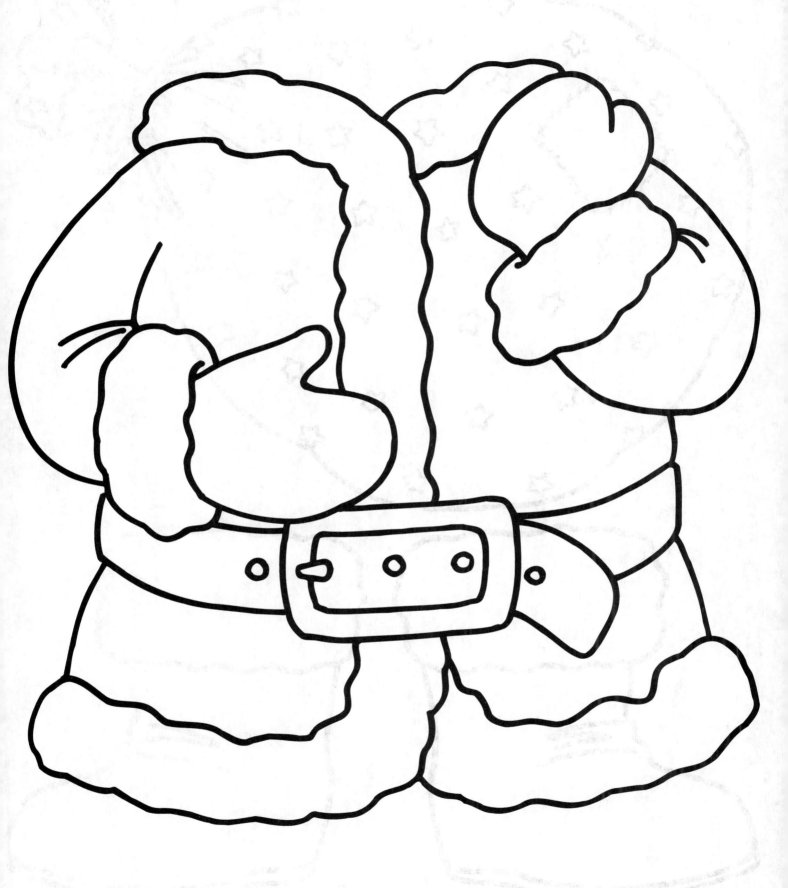

Santa Sack and Boots Patterns

SANTA SONG
(sung to the tune of "She'll Be Comin' Round the Mountain")

Children can place their hand inside the Santa puppet (see page 55) **and manipulate** it as they sing and act out the actions in the following song.

He'll be comin' round for Christmas when he comes,
He'll be comin' round for Christmas when he comes,
He'll be comin' round for Christmas,
He'll be comin' round for Christmas,
He'll be comin' round for Christmas when he comes!

Other verses include:

He'll be ridin' with his reindeer when he comes…

He'll be carryin' lots of toys when he comes…

He'll be wavin' to the children when he comes…

He'll be climbin' down the chimney when he comes…

He'll be laughin' "ho-ho-ho" when he comes…

Help Santa find the way from his house to his sleigh.

Name

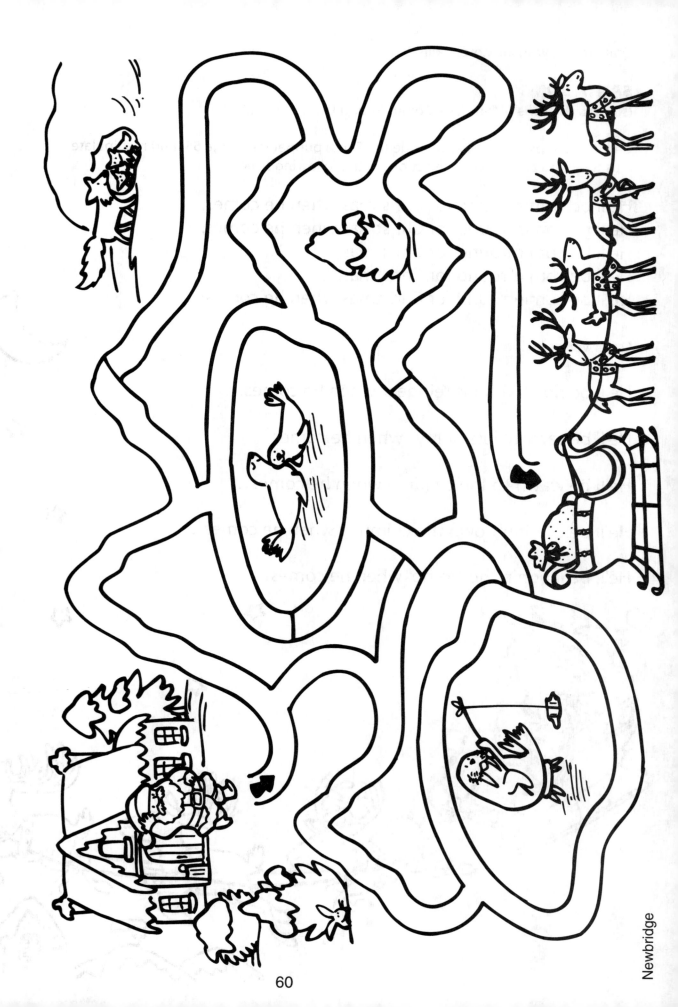

Newbridge

REINDEER STICK PUPPETS

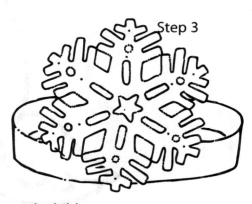

1. Reproduce the reindeer pattern on page 62 once for each child. Have children color all the reindeer and cut out.
2. Tape a tongue depressor or popsicle stick onto the back of each reindeer's head and neck for support. Then tape another tongue depressor on each reindeer to complete the stick puppets.
3. Read the story of Rudolph the Red-Nosed Reindeer aloud to your class. Let children use the stick puppets to act out the story.
4. Use the story as a springboard for talking about individuality. Help children recognize that each person is unique, just like Rudolph, and that is what makes the world so interesting.
5. Tell children that reindeer are used for things other than pulling Santa's sleigh. Use a map to show the class Lapland, the northern portions of Norway, Sweden, Finland, and the Kola peninsula of the Soviet Union. Tell the class that some Laplanders are like cattle farmers, except they herd reindeer instead of cattle. Since reindeer are not kept on farms, the Laplanders must follow the herds of reindeer wherever they go. Reindeer are very strong and are capable of pulling heavy loads for miles.
6. Have children use the stick puppets to make up their own stories about reindeer.

SNOWFLAKE CROWNS

You need:
• crayons or markers
• scissors
• glue
• glitter
• 2" x 24" strips of white construction paper
• stapler

1. Reproduce the snowflake pattern on page 20 once for each child. Have children color the snowflakes and cut out.
2. Ask children to decorate their snowflakes by gluing glitter onto them.
3. Give each child a 2" x 24" strip of white construction paper. Staple the snowflake to the middle of the strip, as shown. Then staple the ends together to fit around each child's head.
4. For activities, see Reindeer and Snowflake Counting Game on page 63.

Reindeer Pattern

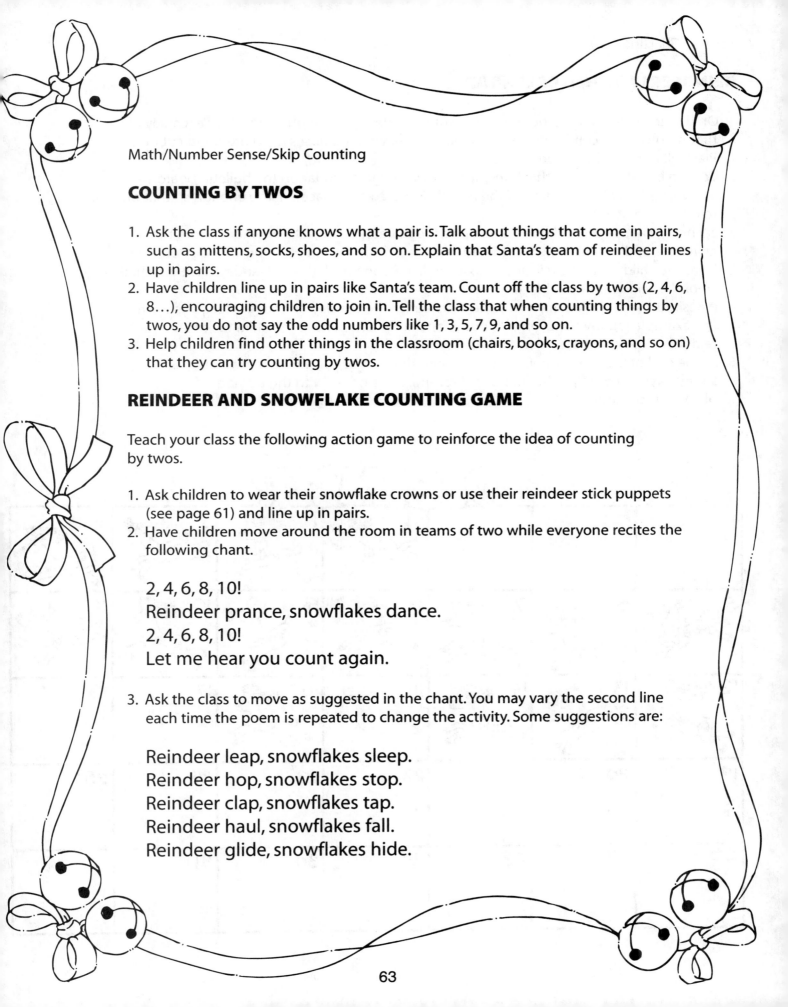

Math/Number Sense/Skip Counting

COUNTING BY TWOS

1. Ask the class if anyone knows what a pair is. Talk about things that come in pairs, such as mittens, socks, shoes, and so on. Explain that Santa's team of reindeer lines up in pairs.
2. Have children line up in pairs like Santa's team. Count off the class by twos (2, 4, 6, 8…), encouraging children to join in. Tell the class that when counting things by twos, you do not say the odd numbers like 1, 3, 5, 7, 9, and so on.
3. Help children find other things in the classroom (chairs, books, crayons, and so on) that they can try counting by twos.

REINDEER AND SNOWFLAKE COUNTING GAME

Teach your class the following action game to reinforce the idea of counting by twos.

1. Ask children to wear their snowflake crowns or use their reindeer stick puppets (see page 61) and line up in pairs.
2. Have children move around the room in teams of two while everyone recites the following chant.

2, 4, 6, 8, 10!
Reindeer prance, snowflakes dance.
2, 4, 6, 8, 10!
Let me hear you count again.

3. Ask the class to move as suggested in the chant. You may vary the second line each time the poem is repeated to change the activity. Some suggestions are:

Reindeer leap, snowflakes sleep.
Reindeer hop, snowflakes stop.
Reindeer clap, snowflakes tap.
Reindeer haul, snowflakes fall.
Reindeer glide, snowflakes hide.

REINDEER WEATHER CALENDAR

1. On the first day of December, reproduce one reindeer pattern on page 62 for each day of that month. Have children color each reindeer, leaving the noses uncolored, and cut out. Place all reindeer in a large envelope.

2. Cover a bulletin board with white paper. Draw a large calendar on the bulletin board, as shown, and number the days of the month. Be sure each space is large enough so that one reindeer can fit inside it.

3. Each day, choose one child to come up to the bulletin board, take a reindeer from the envelope, and describe the weather for that day. If it is snowing, raining, or foggy outside, have the child color the reindeer's nose red like Rudolph's. If it is a clear day, have the child color the reindeer's nose black.

4. If desired, use a black marker to write the weather for the day on the reindeer, as shown (for example, "sunny," "snowing," "cloudy," and so on). Then have the child tack the reindeer in place on the calendar bulletin board.

5. At the end of the month, help children count the number of snowy, rainy, cloudy, and sunny days, or compare the number of red-nosed reindeer with the number of black-nosed reindeer.

DECEMBER

			1 WARM	2 SUNNY	3 COLD	4 COLD
5 FOGGY	6 FOGGY	7 CLEAR	8 COLD	9 WINDY	10 WARM	11 SNOW
12 SNOW	13 SNOW	14 SNOW	15 COLD	16 COLD	17	18
19	20	21	22	23	24	25
26	27	28	29	30	31	

HOLIDAY ORNAMENTS

You need:
- crayons or markers
- scissors
- glue
- tissues or shredded newspaper
- hole puncher
- glitter, ribbons, buttons
- 8" lengths of yarn

1. Reproduce the ornament patterns on page 66 twice for each child. Have children color and cut out.
2. Ask each child to turn the ornaments facedown. Show children how to put glue around the sides and bottom edges of each ornament, leaving a 2" opening across the top.
3. Have children press the glued sides of each ornament together, as shown.
4. After the glue has dried, give each child a tissue or a small handful of shredded newspaper. Help children stuff their ornaments lightly, as shown.
5. Have children glue the tops of the ornaments closed. After the glue has dried, help each child punch a hole near the top of each ornament.
6. Give children decorating materials, such as glitter, ribbons, buttons, and so on, to use to personalize their ornaments.
7. Help children tie 8" lengths of yarn through their ornaments. Let children hang the ornaments on a classroom tree or from the ceiling.

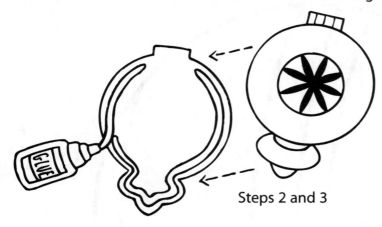

Steps 2 and 3

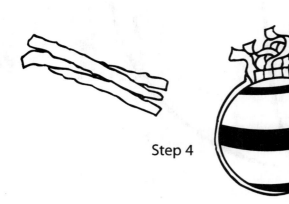

Step 4

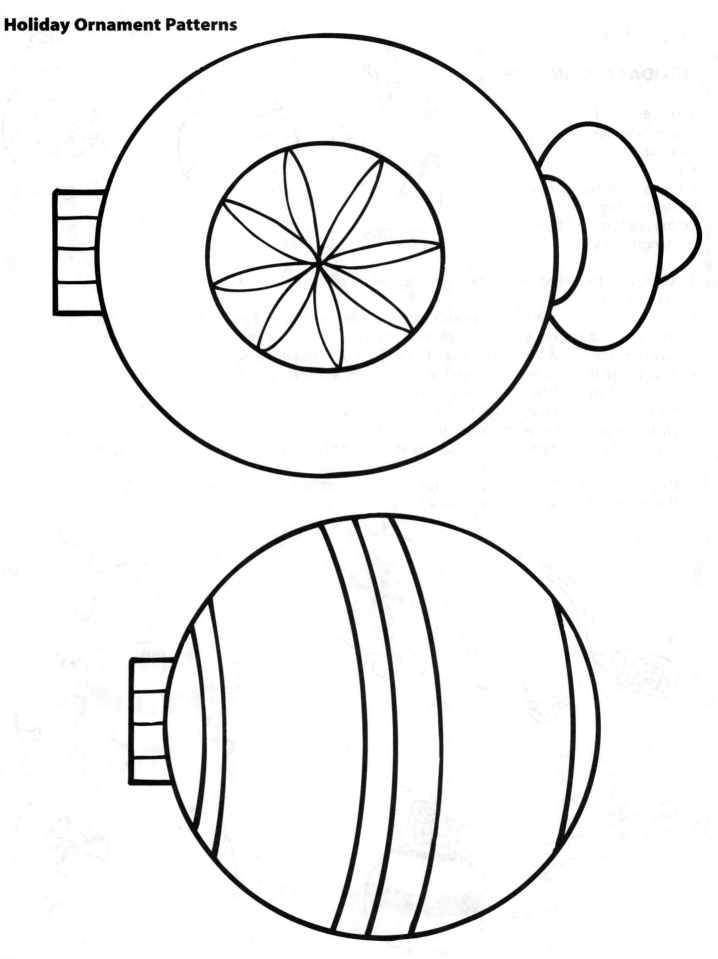

CHRISTMAS MICE DECORATIONS

You need:
• crayons or markers
• scissors
• glue
• tissues or shredded newspaper
• buttons and sequins
• hole puncher
• 8" lengths of yarn

1. Reproduce the mice patterns on page 68 twice for each child. Have children color one copy of each mouse and then cut out all the figures.
2. Have each child glue the printed side of the uncolored mouse to the back of the colored mouse, as shown. Tell each child to leave a 2" opening at the bottom of each mouse.
3. After the glue has dried, have children stuff the mouse with tissues or shredded newspaper and glue closed, as shown.
4. Encourage children to decorate their mice using buttons and sequins for eyes and noses.
5. Tell each child to punch a hole at the top of each mouse. Then help each child thread an 8" length of yarn through each mouse to complete the ornament.
6. Children may hang the mice on a classroom tree, or take them home to hang on their family trees.

Step 2

Step 3

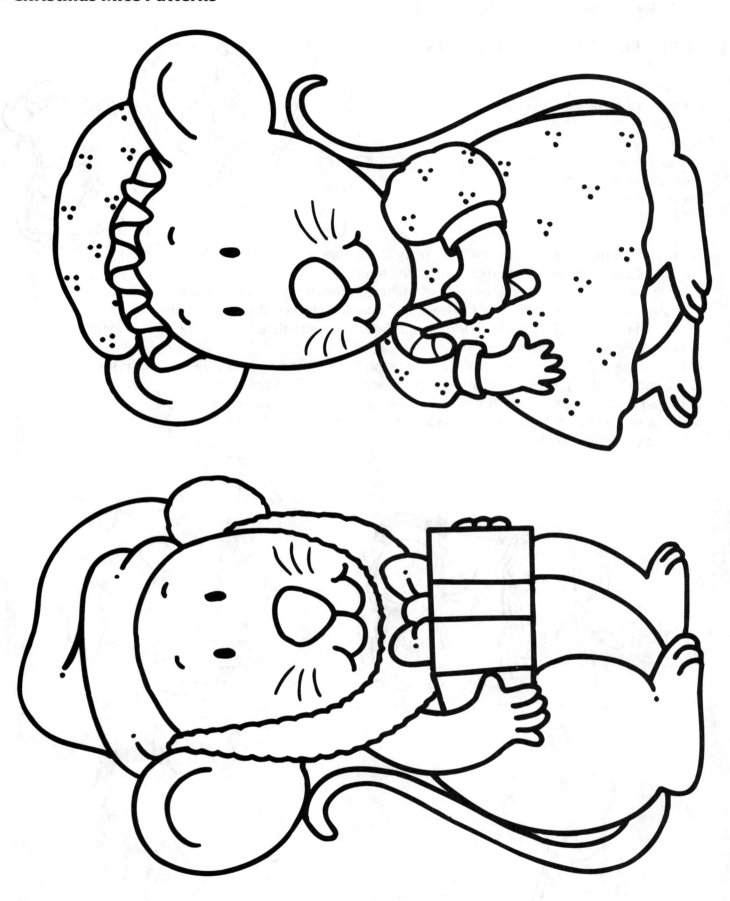

GUESS THE GIFTS

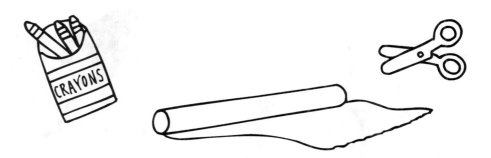

You need:
- magazines and catalogs
- scissors
- pushpins or tacks
- gift wrap
- crayons or markers

1. Cut out pictures of toys, books, and other things children enjoy from magazines and catalogs. Attach the pictures to a bulletin board when children are not in the room.
2. Use a piece of gift wrap to cover each picture, as shown. Tack the gift wrap along the top edge so that the paper may be lifted to reveal the "gift" underneath. You may also wish to tape a bow to each "package."
3. Reproduce the gift tag patterns on page 70 so that there is one tag for each gift. Color the unprinted side of each and cut out.
4. Write two or three words that describe each gift on a tag. For example, if the gift is a bicycle, you may want to write "shiny," "wheels," and "red." Then attach the tags to the appropriate gifts.
5. When children are in the room, have them gather in front of the bulletin board. Read the words on each tag to the class. Then ask volunteers to guess what gift is being described. Have one volunteer come to the bulletin board and lift the gift wrap to "unwrap" the gift.

Gift Tag Patterns

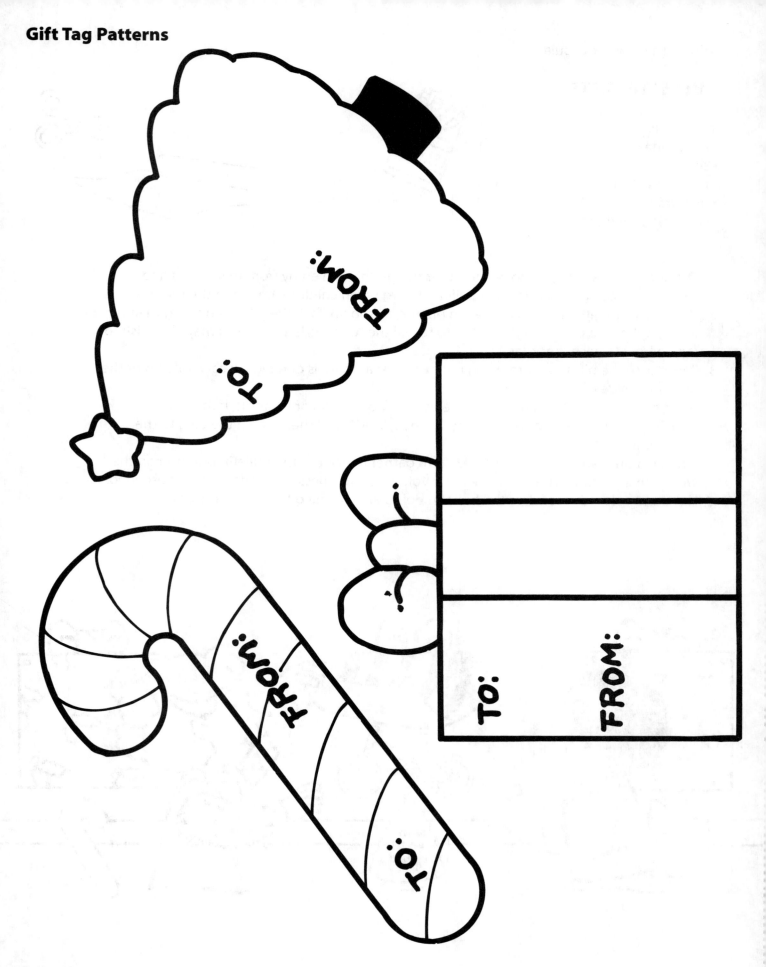

THE VALUES OF KWANZAA

Explain that the holiday of Kwanzaa began in 1966. It was the idea of an African-American college teacher named Dr. Maulana Karenga. He wanted African-Americans to dedicate themselves to seven important values: Sharing, Cooperation, Creativity, Unity, Self-Determination, Purpose, and Faith. He felt that the wintertime, around the beginning of the new year, was an especially good time to think about these values. Kwanzaa lasts from December 26 to January 1.

Each day of Kwanzaa is set aside for one of the seven values. At night, families light one of seven candles in a special candleholder called a *kinara* and talk about the value for that day. In many families, members exchange gifts, especially homemade presents. Near the end of the holiday, the entire neighborhood gets together for a large meal. Traditional African foods are served, and there is lots of singing and dancing.

Encourage children to explain what each of the seven Kwanzaa values means to them. Talk about ways that the values can be practiced—not just in wintertime, but all year long.

Ask children what other values, besides those of Kwanzaa, they feel are important. List their suggestions on the board. You might include some of the following on your list:

• Sharing books   • Solving problems   • Cheering up friends   • Helping with household chores
• Taking turns   • Visiting the sick   • Helping people   • Being courteous

After discussing the values of Kwanzaa, reproduce the pendant symbol patterns on page 79 several times and write one of the value words on each symbol. Display the words where they can be seen and ask children to draw pictures and write or dictate a few sentences about how they might practice one of these values.

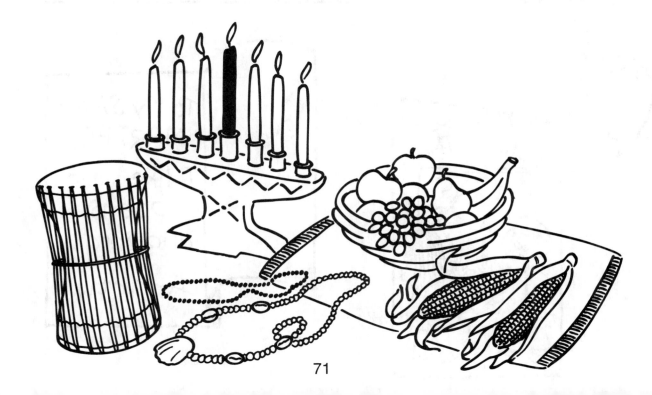

KWANZAA HOLIDAY CARDS

You need:
- scissors
- crayons or markers
- glitter, ribbon, tissue paper
- glue

1. Reproduce one pattern on pages 73 through 75 for each child.
2. Have children color their cards. They may embellish them with glitter, ribbon, brightly colored tissue paper, or other available materials.
3. Have children fold the cards along the center line.
4. On the inside, have each child write or dictate a message to a friend or family member. The message should relate to the picture on the front. (For example: "I like to share with you.")

This card was made by:
Andrew

CREATING

To My Sister MARTHA,
I like your poems and songs.
Andrew

This card was made by: _____

SHARING

CREATING

This card was made by:

COOPERATING

This card was made by: _____

KWANZAA IDEA CHART

You need:
• oaktag
• glue
• markers or crayons

1. Reproduce each pattern on pages 73 through 75 once.
2. Create a large oaktag chart with three columns. At the top of each column paste one of the patterns, as shown.
3. Hold a class discussion in which children suggest specific ways they can share, cooperate, or create. Record their suggestions in the appropriate column on the chart. Sign their initials after their suggestions.
4. Display the chart on the classroom wall. Encourage children to add more suggestions as they think of them.

KWANZAA PLACE MATS

You need:
• crayons or markers
• scissors
• glue
• 12" x 18" pieces of oaktag
• clear contact paper

1. Reproduce the place mat pattern on page 77 once for each child. Have children color and cut out.
2. Have each child mount his or her place mat onto a 12" x 18" piece of oaktag.
3. Let children decorate their place mats to personalize them. If desired, help children write holiday messages on their place mats.
4. When children are satisfied with their creations, laminate the place mats. Let children use them for a classroom celebration of Kwanzaa, or to give as gifts to family members or friends.

KWANZAA PENDANT NECKLACES

You need:
- crayons or markers
- scissors
- hole puncher
- 24" lengths of yarn

1. Reproduce a sheet of pendant symbol patterns on page 79 for each child. Explain to the class that green, black, and red are the traditional colors of Kwanzaa. Encourage children to use these colors as they decorate the pendants with crayons or markers and cut out.
2. Help each child punch holes in the symbols, as indicated.
3. Have children thread 24" lengths of yarn through the symbols.
4. Help children tie the ends of the yarn together to complete their necklaces.

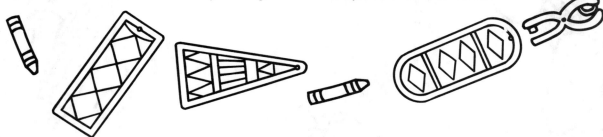

AFRICAN-STYLE HATS

You need:
- scissors
- tape
- crayons or markers
- stapler

1. Reproduce the hat pattern on page 80 twice for each child. Have children cut out and tape the pieces together, as shown, to form a circle.
2. Have children color the hats using bright colors.
3. Show children how to cut slits in the hats by cutting along the dotted lines.
4. Help children fold the tabs down and staple together along the bottom edge, as shown.
5. Encourage children to wear their hats during a classroom Kwanzaa celebration.

Step 4

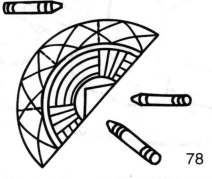

Step 1

Kwanzaa Pendant Symbol Patterns

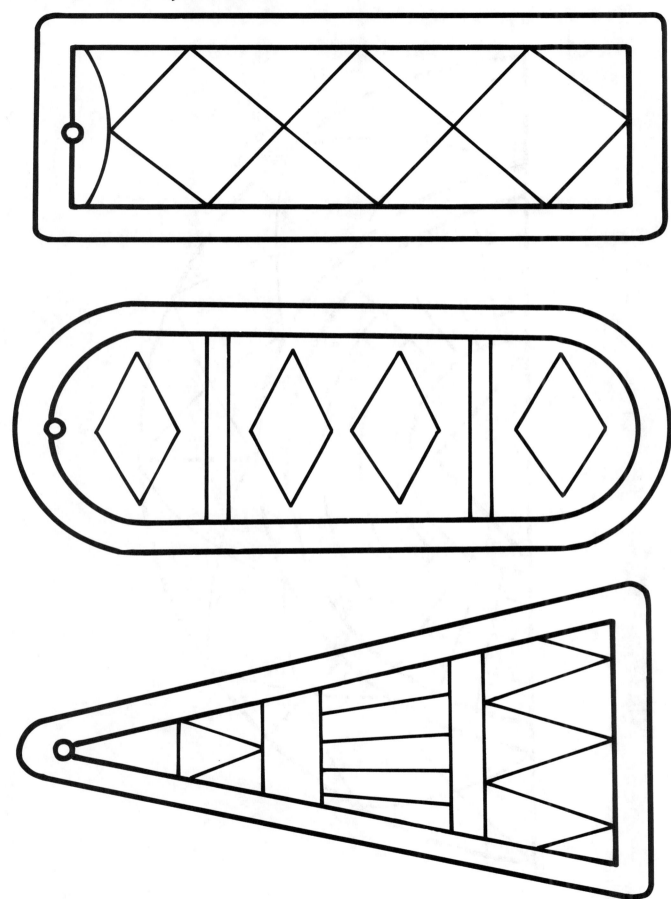

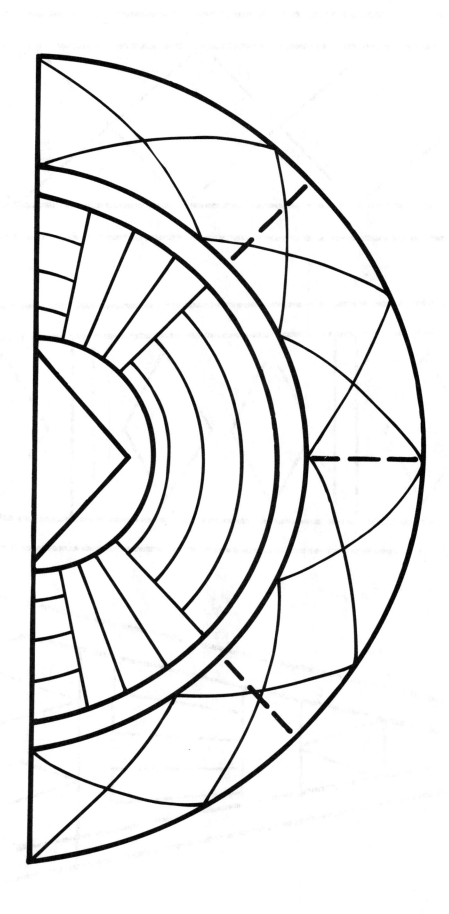